MW01599681

SOUL

WORDS

Reine Amode

PublishAmerica
Baltimore

ISBN: 1-4137-7499-7
PUBLISHED BY PUBLISHAMERICA, LLLP
www.publishamerica.com
Baltimore

Printed in the United States of America

This book is for my biggest inspirations
Simon Lebon
Nick Rhodes
Roger Taylor
John Taylor
Andy Taylor

Thank you to all who have encouraged me and stuck
by me writing this book

SOUL
WORDS

Looking out at the fearless ship
Her masses sway in the wind
Her destiny I believe, Is to sail the liquid sky
Leaving the earth behind
To breathe her life, Onto unfamiliar shores.
Under falling stars
With grace, And furious seas
She steadies me, She humbles me
Floating on the deep blue serenity
Wondrous mistress
Oceans temptress.
I am at your mercy
As you know me so well.
Calling me endlessly
To sail the horizons
Of possibility

As I am fading
Through this ancient evening
I give in to
My shallow breathing
The cities gleaming
With an empty feeling
As I stare out my window
The faces blur
Can I be this numb
While the outsides screaming
With violent echoes
And neon dreaming
I notice my reflection
In the car door mirror
and behind the irony
Is just imagination
An interpretation
A simple me

You have found me through the eons
This soul has been searching
endlessly
God's quest for us has been fulfilled
As I lie here
Fallen to my knees
your warm light of salvation
Engulfs me
I cannot speak

You're more beautiful
Then I would have known
I feel our light expanding outward
And pulling us in
Pure healing
Come onto me
Our polarity is simplicity
At last we are one
To last the eons

The face in the mirror
Challenges my ego
Questions my confidence
Looks familiar
The voice in my head
Acts as an echo
From a cerebral journal
Written in pondiculation
My fascination
My indiscretions
Halo my pupils, my deep meditation
I chalk it up
To quantum physics
As I notice the years
That outline my eyes
I step back
And honor the reflection
And generations smile

Blue melts to white
She craves your eyes
She holds your mind
Energy of light
Element of fire
Bending shadows
Outlined shapes
Lend way to collective silence

Tantric pulsations
Warm vibrations
Don't make her your enemy
Heat rises
Follow it
Understand her grasp
Watch her dance
She's velvet to your eyes

Two, the number of perfection
Equation of existence
What was one
Sought eons for it's completion
Two is balance
Action and reaction
Energy flow
What was one
Knew only silence
A solitary vision
A flat surface
Never ending
Science found it's soul
Took what was whole
Infused an idea and from that came two
With a mind of it's own

The universe became diverse
One orbited the first
They made a perfect circle
Creation was admired
Two became infinity
This is the story of
Molecular design
Searching for an answer
To the meaning of a life

Don't tell secrets
Tension is redemption
Racing thoughts
Eyes of glass
Lips of gloss
So hard to smile

Nylon ecstasy
Feeling electricity
Stir your drink
It will help you think
Temptations creeping
She knows your kink
Does that make you feel dirty?

Can you loathe and lust
Wanting to trust
What inner violence
Makes you break your silence
Too bad she's walked away

The crimson tide
Rolls to shore
And I stand in her anger
As my blood turns warm
The sky over head
Casting shadow puppets
On the sand
And you take my hand
And run your fingers
Through my hair
A mouth like venom
Claims my breath
Tasting the salt
From the seeds of my lips
And every movement
Is outlined by the sun
Feeding my soul
can you make me whole
I am infinite
And your will is blind
We lay entwined
Moist from sin
I gave you my body
But never my mind

Do you remember how to simply feel joy
How to let things go
So your spirit grows
Can you pass no judgment
On others' choices
And listen to the voices of our souls guides
Do you have reverence for life
Does it pass you by
Can you let go of pride
So your heart will survive
Do you know who you really are
Have you come that far
Can you find the bliss
In knowing we exist for a purpose
All of this is a lifetime's gift
A chance to change
Know it's never to late
This is only the beginning
Of the ever after

Take this life
For what it is
Sometimes profound
With every movement
A surreal quest
A mind in distress
And it makes no sense
To cry over it

A world gone numb
Flashing before my eyes
Like a movie screen
In every scene…I read between the lines
Just to survive

You're just like a child
Exploring. exclaiming
But time brings change my friend
You have to embrace the essence
Remember all the moments
And know this.

It's reverence that brings us bliss
If we could seal it with a kiss
If you could hold it in your hands
As it slips away like sand

And look into these eyes
I've never told you lies
Was hope that made us high
Always remember

Sometimes you have to step back
And let fate take it's hand
If there is nothing left to give
When you can barely stand
When the grains of sand
Slip through your finger tips
Do not try and grasp it

When the smiles hurt
And the faces seem to stare
When you cannot care anymore
Close your eyes
Let the tears make you blind
But realize this

There is really a purpose
And if you learn acceptance
You could dance on Hallowed ground
Make the world go round
And without a sound
When you've fallen to your knees
Like the soul inside should bleed
Remember who you are
And how you got this far
Time will always heal
Just let your spirit feel
And give your soul it's mercy

I feel the hum
Burning in my ears
The sounds of metal
Crashing on the tar
Helpless I stare
And faster they run
And my breath gets lost
On the screams of unbelief
And terror turns to numb
A child's eyes, turn like glass
And time stands still
As the skyline falls
And the world watches. Our every step
Heaven cries. And angels bow
In silence
Fear
Runs in rivers of blood
Shed from hate
Yet we share the same air
Nothing will be the same
Will we ever feel safe
Fallen into grace
We survive
But can never replace,. what's been lost
The day
The city was on fire

I close my eyes
And the whispers outside
Seem to fade
The thoughts stream in from yesterday
So I drink the poison cup
Hoping I will feel numb
If I stay away
Will you change
If I keep this up
I will self destruct
Will they remember my name
Can you die from shame
Why did I let things go this way
I look at my life
Through tainted eyes
Lost in a world
I don't recognize
It's a sacrifice
A bitter price to pay
I can only take it
Day by day
Strangers know my name
Read me like a book
Take a closer look
And I walk away

Light prisms searching through the trees
Stretch across the floor
And shadows on my door
In a sky that holds the storm
Your words to keep me warm
Autumn turns the breeze
So bitter in the dark
The harvest moon is changing
The lives it's rearranging
Later starts the morning
Autumn is adorning
It's colors on the earth
Such a subtle birth
Of long tranquility
All washed over me
My apple cider dreams
Dancing in the leaves
Light

A simple reminder
That time
Has humbled me

I close my eyes
As the rhythm changes
I feel the vibrations
Running my brain
My body sways
To the eclectic haze
Come dance with me
In this tribal maze

You feed my imagination
Your indiscretions
Our culmination
You whisper to me

I feel the blood drain
And my body is alive
Your scent enslaves me
And your body is fire

Can you taste the exchange
Will you be the same
Your mind at my mercy
As I walk away

Gray sky above me
In her blistering rage
Let down your tears
And I'll dance in your rain
The tempting of fate
A hollow exchange
A promise made
I won't be the same

Lips so gently I seek
A secret I must keep
Your fever runs within me
Burning my veins
As the tides change
Your light rolls in

Under my skin
You set me free
So close
Yet too far to reach
All I can do
Is breathe

You're the scent of sin
And you draw me in
Temptation swells
Now you know me well
Let me go

He sees through her narcissistic ways
And laughs as she gets frustrated
The crowds gaze her up and down
She looks at her face
When no ones around
N.Y has her wrapped up in pavement
So used and spent
Days come and went
Even the friends have walked away
Not knowing what to say
The family she's left behind
Stay close in her mind
He is serious
But kind to her
A woman some call mother
A weekend lover
Chasing a dream
She is not what she seems
And he breaks her chain
Takes the anger and pain
Holds up the mirror
To her blinded eyes
This is what I see
He whispers
A fragmented reflection
And the world swallows me

Reality exists
In nocturnal bliss
The moments we notice
Just days like this
Where nothing is heavy
To hang on your head
Stretched across my bed
Lazy and spent

As you smile at me
Familiar eyes see
I am just glad to be
Next to you

I can't help but notice
The scent of your skin
As I take you in
And you comfort me
No where to be
Just easy and free
Make love to me
Till this Sunday ends

In my complex space
No one knows me
I see you reading my face
Looking for answers
Say something brilliant
Why try and impress me
Who am I really
Who do you think I should be
It gets tiring for me
My colorful facade
Can turn to gray so quickly
I had listened to all that they say
Do you think I would break
So easy to judge me
We all make mistakes
Would that turn you away
If I was simple or vague
Give what you take
Respect and faith
Leave your mind blank
When you approach me
And listen
In honesty

Today you looked at me
With innocent eyes
Till the years of fear shown through
Just a child
Left for death
Shattered and confused
Broken and abused
And I beg the powers that be
To guide me to your mercy
To show me how to heal thee
All the shame I see
Written on your face
A child of disgrace
They made you feel this way
Time will heal no wounds
The nightmares take you soon
I hold you with my soul
And try to keep you whole

Listen to the angels sing
Child you are everything
I blanket you from an angry face
A fathers fist
A mothers hate
and till this day
You are in my grace
I watched you grow
And on your own
The smiles
Say it all

I dream in colors
I feel emotions in black and white
My mind is endless
My thoughts are relentless
I don't let many people reflect in my eyes
I like to taste their energy first
Beautiful soul to quench my thirst
You must listen, to my whispered words
Never a fear for sentiment
A dreamer knows a dreamer
And sorrow collects fools
I've not come face to face
With anyone who knew
I am bewildered and tied in knots
My visions in shambles
But it's all I've got
I sort, with a hope to find
Because negative thinking is suicide
Brick by brick I'm building a mind
Each moment I've collected
I am
Leaving behind
Simple
Yet sublime

Miles away at the edge of the shore
There is a tower that stands with the sky
Stones put together with skin and bone
Held together with rare earth
A temple to the ocean
The wind spirals around her peek
I see the stories she holds close
I see the lives lost before her
They paint her
Or ignore her
And she weeps
Sending her moans over the hallow sea
She beckons me
My thoughts twisting in ivy
Climbing endlessly
Pulling me towards the blue tranquility
This is my lady of envy
My words give her ephemeral peace
As I give miles of land to my feet
I turn back
Just once
To keep her with me

I awaken to an aching
Plains of reality ease me into breath
Noon is rising above my head
The night came and went
The smell of ginger graces my pillow
And my hands
Slowly I remember
Where you touched me
The room feels like it's closing in
Laughter passes my windows ledge
I watch the shadows from the trees
Stretch across my bed
The day came and went
I could only lay there
Confused and spent
Going over in my thoughts
Step by step
what it meant to me
I left the phone ringing
And I drift to sleep
Tomorrow
Is my sanctuary

Do not ponder who I am
Do not question my moral path
Do not invade my personal space
I am a human
Not just a face
What gives you the right
To chastise me
You feel you know
It's just what you see
I've paved my road
I will find my way
I live with my self
Everyday
Don't dig to deep
There is nothing to know
Accept what I give
And leave things alone

This body shivers
As the blue dawn rises
Outlining years that wait before me
I raise a trembling hand
To trace a rosy cast, Along a fading past
That drips behind me
Naked I stand, and from deep within
I am set free
In touch, Yet so out of reach
The suns heat, Paints the illusion of rivers flowing
Towards the endless horizon
Nothing is wet, but me
Blinded by the steam
That seeps beneath my feet
So I scream
My ashes blow across the open
I have found unity

One step
Just one breath
Another day
That you can grasp
Because in this life
We forget to live
We learn to take
Yet hardly give

I might be the one
To carry on..
But you were strong
Though that breath is gone
You still belong in my world

One truth
Just a simple tool
Another year
That you never knew
Because in this life
We must make things right
Learn to heal
And let go of fear

I might be the one
To carry on..
But you were strong
Though that breath is gone
You still belong in my world

Three simple words
Make sure they are heard
Whisper them if you must
And do not just believe
They really knew

What bitter pill did you swallow
What makes a heart so hollow
What did you hope to achieve
Is this how you want to live?

Not all people are the same
Direct the words where the anger's to blame
You're only destroying yourself
Loathing will just pin you down
There will always be fear before trust
But to live in your past and disgust
Is imprisoning your soul...

We were all meant to grow
Learn from mistakes as a whole
This is the reality of life
We hear not always what we like
But you have to understand
And respect every gentile hand
That reaches out

Harmony is what it's all about
You can disagree with me
Yet exist peacefully in the same space
Pride can only save face for awhile
So open up your mind and smile
Understand another view
And remember
The polarity of truth

Soft and warm it envelops me
Driving harder on the pavement
It washes away the indifference
Not like I would try to save it
I run my finger on the window pane
And trace my memories out of the rain
Remembering days…when things were plain
It's not who I am now…
Don't think I could take it

Seeing how the water gathers
Collective lights on the top
Making patterns
Fitting my mood
As my mind is all scattered
Children play the in streaming matter
Dancing like fairytales
Surrendering to the moment
And now I own it
And it just gets better

Today, unlike many others
I had to make a choice
What life means to me
Seems most days
It's very lonely
I sometimes wonder am I the only one
Who doubts what I believe
Is there really a destiny we reach
Will somebody really see
All that's inside of me
It's a give and take
We bend
Not brake
It will never be easy
Love seems so silly
What is it honestly
Emotion in a shallow world
A fairytale read to a little girl
Something we all need
We want to feed the soul
And watch it grow
And who really knows
What the future brings

To the light, I hold the glass jar
What's inside, I am wondering
A child's whisper
Says follow me
Give in to your wonder, and make believe
The pictures come so vividly
As it bends my vision
And colors dance
I think of you, with innocence
How I wish I could give you this
Your mind needs a place to rest
Compassionate and comforting glass
On my shelf, and I never noticed
All the things you could be
I took for granted, your emptiness
And always filled it
Flowers will never do you justice
I now see this
As I forgot you were simply glass
As the prisms of colors dance on my walls
I see the gift you gave me
Of memories

In your hostility
In your loathing for me
I see an insecurity
Could it be
Just an insensitivity
In your choice of words
In your plan to hurt
Do you find relief
As you belittle me
It gave me a chance to see
Inside your personality
In your unhappiness
In your heads a mess
One day you will regret
One day you'll look inside
As you reflect on life
And there will be an emptiness
A world out of focus
A face you hardly notice
A soul
Who's very lonely

As I'm looking down
At the moving ground
Closing my mind
To the world that surrounds
In my head
There's a whispering sound
It seduces me
And turns me out
Faces gather, in the back of my thoughts
And I find myself looking, at the life I bought
Wondering years
Blissful sights
Reaching, for the feeling
It's a compromise
Yet I try to understand
Where the last footstep ends
And the new ones began

Where are the simple days
Of last
People seem to live in the past
Holding on to memories
Broken hearts
And shattered dreams
What's left for one to believe in

A simple request
In a world out of focus
When life is a mess
And you feel like no one will notice
If you disappear

When you're drowning in your fears
Of never living up to
What you hear you should be
When staring into space
Or blankly at a face
Is your reality

You have to break away
Give your mind some space
Remind yourself to breathe
Find your will again
Never turn around
Make peace with what you've found

What comes from all of this
When tears have stained your face
When it all seems out of place
And you try to run away

It follows you

Until you break

And all that you can do
Is live for today
Find your solid ground
And simply be

Stare up into the big blue sky
And lose your troubles here
Spinning round in circles
Letting go of fear

This light can be contagious
I find your love courageous
It's all that's left to save us
Let envy disappear

Let go and lose yourself
This day's like nothing else
Breathe deep and let it out
Listen to the rhythm inside yourself

We all send vibrations
It's what makes the soul
And if you look directly
You might miss it all

So close your eyes and listen
Feel the hum that sends you bliss
And dance to the music you keep inside you
Let your peaceful mind exist

The form took shape
Like a masterpiece
As I watched you from a distance
The sheer essence of man
Challenging his master plan
This body is a temple
And he pushes further from the sand
Drenched in power and determination
Riding the high with every movement
Exhilaration...in it's purest form
True beauty
I am in awe
And this will carry you
In this life

Early morn
Break of dawn
Lights above the pavement still glow
The hush of the world drones
A deep sigh
A nocturnal high
Drawing on the last
Of the energy flow
Just let go
Drift to sleep
And in those hours
Will you think of me
An absent heart
Miles apart
Burning in my mind
Are the days of last
As the sun finds the sky
And life should call
Reminding you simply
There is more to it all
Than the whispers of the night

Humanity sharing space
We have come along way
From the wayward days of hate
Feeding minds with knowledge
The lives we lead don't segregate

The future seems opaque
Keep your faith
And do not be afraid
Knowing everything
Can take the lesson away

Violence and anger
In the face of a stranger
Do not judge
What you cannot see

Politics and religion
The color of skin
The languages of the universe
We are all made of earth
Fire and rain
What makes you think
Is what makes you the same

He was left with no words
His mouth formed whispers
Nothing really heard
So the world ignored him
And they named him slow

So ready they were
To take the hope from his eyes
So willing to learn
So hard he would try
So many nights mommy cried
For his life to be bright

what they seemed to overlook
All the steps that he took
All the times he would fall
He was not ashamed to crawl

It was they who hid their faces
Reading charts, comparing his disgrace
As he smiled at them in compassion
But there was no reaction
From the blind

Little boy
Take your little steps
Whisper your words
Know you are heard
There is hope in your heart
There is strength in your mind
Just take your time
And learn how you can
The mistakes of man
Are not your burden

Mommy is proud

Let the mind go
Your solitary journey will flow
Heal on it's own

Close your eyes
It's energizing to breathe deep
Lose your soul in a nocturnal feast
Of vibrations and colors
In vivid dreams

Your quest for peace
Must simply be
Creation is beauty
It holds the key

What you've always been
From beginning to end
A simple man
Complicated by your mind
Distracted and blind
Now the channels opened
And you are free

It was powerful
Yet subtle
Colors shining in the purest form
They cling to the mind
And made each breath, ephemeral

There is a freedom in reverence
Quiet bliss enters the chaotic mess
We call life
So simple is this, taken for granted
What we do not understand
Should not be missed

We climb out of fear
We reach for knowledge
Experience becomes a canvas
Wisdom is the form it takes
Turning emotions into pictures

Abstract portraits
Deep vibrations
Incarnation
I see your transformation
You are inspiration to me
Change, is what makes the soul thrive

The imperfections of a human nation
Brought to the surface
With the modern day segregation
Hypocrites, lunatics and fascists writing speeches
Trying to teach us and force feed us
What is education, in an angry nation
Nothing left for imagination or creation
Take this for what it is

Point fingers in a house of glass
See how fast the masses come to the rescue
Everyone's got answers, But no one knows what to do
Talk is cheap in a world of over indulged haikus
Everyone's been abused
Everyone's been bruised
Not a day goes by that someone does not cry
I am a victim of the system
To anyone who will listen
Take this for what it is

Pop icons rule the world
Coffee table reading is in the classrooms
The internet is that little pill
So hard to swallow
So many follow blindly
Take this for what it is

Intellect in retrospect
Can fall short in the wrong hands
This does not make the man
Serial killers can have high IQ's
See this everyday in the news
Take this for what it is

All we are told, life's evolution
We can fill it with fear and disillusion
You can spend it judging and searching truths
In the end you will look in the mirror
And it will still be you
Take this for what it is

We are flesh and bone
As humanity toils the earth
From the time of birth
Creation has been on a mission
To seek perfection

Complicated by opinion
We regress
Tolerance is the first step
To understand.

We reap what we sow
Karma is nothing you own
It's what you give, how you live
Not who you are
Understand

Life can be complex
If you take it out of context
You have to learn to reflect on yourself
And be open to learn Understand

Less is your burden
When you welcome change
To observe without judging
To love without fear
To strive
To understand

As you lay sleeping
In your comfortable space
I trace the years
That outline your face
A fear takes me over
How long will you stay
Will you get to know me
With no games to play

You stir in the daybreak
To an honest mistake
I see it in your eyes
As you look away
I smile and release you
No promises made
And I try to remember
To live for today

The hardest part
Is how I question myself
Can I not be loved
Like everyone else
Then reason takes over
And I write it down
With tears on a page
When no ones around
Hurting, dreaming, wanting, needing.
And now I know myself well

I find myself asking
Is this what is to be
You never get to close to me
Who hurt you that bad
Left you in this mess
Jaded you confess
Eyes full of regret

[chorus]
Do you know what's real?
Are you so afraid to feel
Open up and heal yourself
Do you know how to let go...

We can take our time
Trust is nothing you learn overnight
No claims to what is mine
I let you inside, I made it right
Will you open up your mind and see
I am not the one who held you captive while you
bleed...

[chorus]
Do you know what's real?
Are you so afraid to feel
Open up and heal yourself
Do you know how to let go...

Do you know what you want
Do you own up to the part
Was it real when you let go
She was not the one you know…

Taste
Touch
Smile

This is real

Staring blankly into the faces
The crowd is screaming
But your numb to the feeling
Lights are bright, reflective insight
Be who you are, a superstar
But will it take you far in the light of day

Electric-retro-super-genius
Analyzing all the lyrics
Egocentric-partially plastic
Come to paint the world fantastic

Grasping the dream of glamour and fashion
Filling a void
But it's never lasted
What a big mistake
What a toll it will take
When the image breaks

But then it's too late
And the world is captivated
From an ideal
From nothing real
Are you able to heal
When your numb to feel

At first glance
In the darkness
As the shadows
Caress your eyes
I noticed, keeping quiet
How the pale light
In the distance
Made their color
Look like fire
I had to turn away
So you could not read my mind
As you whisper
In my ear
The words fell on me like sin
And my body came alive

Softly
As your fingers trace my spine
A fever runs over me
And my eyes went blind
Why do you challenge me
While your lips devour me
I smile when you realize
Your will is mine

Have you looked in the mirror
Does the reflection haunt you
Does it show you the person you wish to be
When you sleep at night
Does it give you insight
When you look at your life
Are you buried in pride
If you just let things go
You can heal the inside

Listen to the voice
That echoes in your soul
It will keep you whole
And shine the brightest light
If you just forgive
And try to live
In sincerity
You will soon be free
Of the guilt and shame
And all the pain
Will fade away
And the sun will embrace you
As it falls from the sky
And the colors of the earth
Will stream from your eyes
Love should be blind
Nothing but kind
Just give it time
You can escape the world
But never your mind

It happened all at once
Maybe it was the way you looked at me
I saw something
I never noticed before
It was deep inside your eyes
Years and years of devotion
A soul so full of emotion
A warm smile
Was there all the while
Why could I not have seen this
As the years went by
We grew close in our comfortable space
So sad that we are walking away
Two lives that changed
Memories time cannot erase
Always remember
There will always be a place for you
In the woman I became

Open wounds
On the inside
Tearing at memories
Falling apart
Where do I start
How do I let go
Would you even know
All these years
A thousand tears
I look in your eyes
And you disappear
I see your fear
How do I let go
It's the only life I know
The mess you left behind
Now is mine
To pick up the pieces
To make sense of what's wasted
There is anger and hatred
I hope time will fade it
So I can replace it
With life and peace
As I walk away
And close this door
The hardest thing
I have ever done
I move on
And with my heart
I wish you love

As I look into my senses
To find all of the answers
I cannot help but wander
Looking for the muse

In my deepest hours
Twisting in your mercy
My soul fills up with colors
As your taking me

Temporal in surrender
Your whispers take me over
Dare I let you follow
And see into this mind

Was at last evening
Warm and inviting
The taste of salt water
Lays heavy in the air

Dancing above the trees
A summer breeze
Caresses the moon
Entwined in lightening
Your whispers tantalizing

Are you really there

Your shadows trace my every movement
The silence is haunting
As it seduces my mind
Your lips taste of envy
And your will is blind

Yet I know you will follow
Your curiosity is on fire

They cannot touch you
Because you'll break
I always give
You always take
What a mistake

You're mirror eyes
Hypnotize
Can't be yourself
When you're with someone else
I watch you grovel
In you're sorrows and drink
And what do you think
Will come of this
Now everyone knows
You're a fake

Quiet unfolds, in my starving soul
As the vibrations of tranquility
Guide me on
Peace of mind
I long to find
Leaving an angry world behind

I am mesmerized
As my breath runs deep
Eyes growing heavy
I drift to sleep

And you speak to me
In rhythm and rhyme
Hushing my lips
Softly a kiss
Losing myself to a Zen like bliss

As eyes open wide
Visions fragmented
You're just a figment
Of imagination

My name is solitude
Not to be confused with loneliness
I am the mistress of your peaceful soul
I am here to keep you whole
When you need to let go
When the pain runs deep
And your visions are scattered
When ending life
Does not seem to matter
I lay at your feet
As you seek for mercy
As you fall to your knees
I will wipe the tears
Through all these years
I will stand here
In your shadows
To whisper you kindness
As a simple reminder
You are loved

Inside I believe
We all have a child.
Frightened and helpless to who we've become
Shameful repression is easy for some
I love this child
So deep inside
This heart sees life
Through innocent eyes.
This child holds my memories
That gets lost in my world.
And catches my tears
When this voice is not heard.
I need this child to guide my way.
To reckless abandonment
When my mind gets frayed
We should cherish these children
That live deep inside
Their are only hope
In our will to survive

Close your eyes
My sweet divine
As I trace my fingers
Across your spine
Your will is treacherous
My lust sublime
Turmoil whispers
She know you well
Your conscience quickens
Will she kiss and tell
Your lips explore me
In a frenetic exchange
The waves of pleasure, Engulf me
As I remain untamed

Come and visit me
In these hours of last I weep
Lay next to me
And sleep.
Let me cover you with peace.
Come and sit with me
Lift your weary head and see
In the morning hush I'd be
Come and touch my lips with yours
As I ask of nothing more.
In the days of last adored
Was a yearning scorned.
Quietly, I trace
With my eyes along a face
As I search with hopes to find
The man inside the mind
Come and take me in
I feel your breath and taste your skin
I expect nothing more
Entwined in linen
On the floor

Mistress lady
I am divine
Lustful, sexual, my blood is wine
Whisper my name
And your body is mine
Nightfall crawls across your walls
Open up your window pane
In the shadows
I wait for your call
I am here to taste my claim
I am pleasure
I am desire
I am in your veins
I burn like fire
In your sleep
I torment your dreams
Cum
Then feel my mystery
You cannot escape this fever I give you
Do you dare to challenge me
Mistress lady I am divine
I whisper your name
And your body is mine

I am the momentary silence
I am the aftermath of violence
I come to numb the pain
I am the picture frame of your life
This fear is closing all the doors
These scars are prisoners of war
The shame is like none you have known before
How could this be a part of me you say
Why did I let it go this way
Where was my angel in disguise
The tears that burn inside these eyes
Don't hate, The world in not your crutch
Don't wait, time only heals so much
Trust, A word I rarely use
Child, She was abused
Let it heal
The pain is real
Each day you try to feel
Each time you open up your book
Each word you write
You take a closer look, then you find a healing has
started
Believe in yourself
You're not yesterdays child

Here I sit
On a park bench
In the city of circumstance
Feeding pigeons of poverty
Dreaming of a soft cover harlequin romance
Watching the passers by
Making up stories for their lives
I laugh to myself
As I wonder how I seem to someone else
A month ago today
I took a train to a better life
And I worked to survive
Music taking a space on the back shelf of my mind
Scraps of paper fill my pockets
Ideas in rhyme
There scattered but there mine
I look at some faces here
And you can see the years
What did they leave behind
To feast in the city of lights
Their eyes say they tried
A cup of coffee tells a story here
It's a night out
It feeds my imagination
Here on my park bench
I can still smile
Because the vibes are strong yet
And I've just arrived

71

Colors
What are they
Shades of emotion
If everything was clear to us
We would never learn
Maybe that's why
We have so many questions
To color life in
Without color
Everything would fade
Nothing to see
Colors
But to identify uniqueness
Look around
Mans colors
Listen to the colors of music
Life
A color
Claim it
And paint yourself a universe

The beginning is never at the bottom
People always start in the middle
The endless riddle
Cynical in the climb
When you get to the top
Take it all in
There's a steep drop

The air gets you high
Time flies by
People become faces
Memories are just places you've been
No attachments
What makes it relevant

Welcome to the long mile
The stretch of life
Where you learn your lesson
We are above nothing
Just surviving

Collect your templates
Build your bridges
Tie them to your back
And carry them down the hill

Don't forget your will
It's always ten miles down

Do not be afraid
When your mind needs to rest
Come and find your peace
Close your eyes and sleep
Come and catch your breath

Come and be yourself
When there's nothing else
When worry stains your brow
The world can make you drown
Just let me love you

Eyes are washed like glass
Numbing to the touch
Pushing to the limits
Does not give you much

This life can be surreal
Believe in how you feel
Remember that you shine
And always take your time

Do not look away this time
show me your sin
Let your eyes tell all
Crawl under my skin

Feel your heat rise
Come closer to me
Breathe
Smell the challenge
Think I can't see?

Test me
Taste me
You won't break me
Feed your kink
Come and drink me
I like to tease you
But I can please you
So don't look away
Give in and play

It was so strong
But was it real
Some law of the universe
Had made things weird

Cross connection
Caused deep reflection
It feels so surreal
Yet I found some redemption

How does this make you feel

When thoughts flow freely
Do they flow on the same train
Some force of nature
Another plane

Are you toying with me
How can this be
It gives me such chills
Each word I read

Somehow I fear you
I want to be near you
But what if you see
Just like me
The colors and vibrations
Human sensations
Energy
It's just like a dream
What does it mean
It could really be
Nothing

The rings around the sun
Change with the tide
Your quest to see it
Can leave you blind

You have to close your eyes
Bend warm rays
Into soft light
Makes you high
Take your time

The magnetic pull
Equal forces, standing still
Energy
Polarity
Spin on your axis
While your soul relaxes
This is what you do to me

Charkas, red , blue and violet
Keep you grounded
Make your core fall silent
Never fight this
Your will is infinite
In the center of your mind

Young woman, where is your innocence
Gone are the days of playing princess
Now in the eyes of youth
I see truth, to the world that surrounds you.

Young woman, as you're finding yourself
Let lessons guide you
And wisdom find you
Do not sit idle
Always move ahead

Out there I cannot protect you
My only hope
Is you remember
What I have taught you
What your innocence brought you
May you never lose touch
May you never forget
Who you are

Down the long hallway
Counting each step
Doors open, rooms are empty
This is the life that was built by regret

Windows to view the world outside
Stairs to nowhere
Still we climb
The house of sacrifice
Built one brick at a time

A solid foundation
Nails of frustration
Hammered into walls of regression
Shielded with a roof of temptation

We try to sell it when we outgrow the space
To someone who's needy
This life is greedy
We always complain
When the plaster breaks

Down the long hallway
Walked so many times
There's an echo of footsteps
That never were mine

Day break, nothings expected
Warmth from the sun
Collects on my brow
Solitude wrapped in cotton bliss
The taste of you
Will hush my lips

Moisture rises from love stained skin
Close your eyes and take it in
Your fever is scented
With the smell of sin
Nocturnal whispers
Tracing fingers
The moment lingers
As the day begins

Can you hold the mirror of yourself
In the palm of your hand
And from cover to cover, understand
Your master plan

Do the windows of the past
Let in a draft
Blowing the pages
Stirring the imagination
Lets hope this can last

This is when you know
Deep in your soul
Where you stand
What makes you whole
That's hard to swallow
Not easy to follow
Time to let go

Emotions rush over you
Let them through
Scroll them in solitude
Let them heal
Let them make you feel
Your world is surreal
But this is you

Hold the mirror in the palm of your hands
Feed your mind
Yet understand
Words are the reality
Not the face of a man

Hold your breath
This is life
Flowing freely inside you
Do not take for granted
How good it feels
That the soul heals
Even when your blind

Have no regrets
Live with purpose
Even if it hurts us
You never know when it could end

Look in the eyes of your children
Sing in blissfulness
See the world, and make your mark
Make them remember who you are
You only get once chance
So understand
And make amends
With all you can

Let the tears flow
But hold your own
And learn to run
And breathe

What dreams are these of distant lands
Where the sun should rise and bare her fruits
The shores of reality whisper her truths
Here, time is endless
Yet never empty

Shadows cast forward portraits
The goddess of fire gives no mercy
From behind she flames the earth
Melting the horizon
To a crimson rebirth

Tantric fevers rage and dance
Hours pass
Like years and years
I am blind
Yet now I am healed

Silence rings in my ears
Over and over
I hang on your last words
They flow in my veins

And poison my brain
I question your motives
But it still hurts the same

Left in the doorway
Was the life before
Prisms of vivid emotions
Cast down to the floor
Projected and retracted
While my soul was distracted
You burned me once more

I have moved on
Forgiving and living
The anger you hold
Makes your eyes look cold
I follow no shadows
Cause they got you to hold

My eyes wrap around damp roadways
The rain paints pebbles and concrete
Pockets filled with napkins and change
I hurry
For nothing

Stale days and numb nights
Smoke scented hair
I just sit and stair into the crowd
Mixing ice in glass ponderings
The music drowning me

So why am I here
I come out
To disappear
The irony

Footsteps mellow walkway cliques
The night air swallows me
Painted doll
Encased in envy
The City
Made me

Deep crimson
Warm sensations
Touching softly
Your whispers crashing in my brain
Heat rising under skin
Taste your claim

Slowly slipping
Wet and dripping
Vivid portraits
Trace your mind
This is the crimson tide
Her waves trace your spine

The scent of woman
Stains your neck
Standing still
With baited breath
This is crimson envy
She knows who you are

Time and space
Reaching for the milky way
The planets change shape
Eyes like stars
Don't float too far away

Over head
Lights bring the sky closer
We soar
We feed
At intergalactic speeds
You are free in this place

Blue and white
So pure, like electricity
Beyond understanding
A greater being
Heavens never ending
Atmosphere
We belong here
In the galaxy

I watched you with hope
So many years slipped by
You'll never know now
I don't know how
To say goodbye

It's taken all I am
To finally understand
With open hands
I hold them to the sky

How I've been blind
Clouded by fairytales
When all else failed
Something to believe in
Crucified me like nails

Self inflicted sorrow
The time I used was borrowed
With your help, I saw tomorrow
That was then…

I cannot take it back
Though foolish I do feel
An ideal
From nothing real
I give up the hope
Time will heal

This is the only way
I know how
To let go
And say goodbye

She stood in the middle of the stairs
Open hand
Lips swollen from the kiss
Entwined in her breath
A whisper of promise

Afternoon leaves shadows painting her walls
Will he call

Coffee cup canvas
Swirls of milk and sugar high
She stares inside
And remembers

Not really friends
Never lovers
Two stubborn faces
The wrong time
In the same places
Left to always wonder

When he left her standing
In the hall

Tantric thoughts betray blind will
He stands with shallow breath
Warming my fingertips
Sending vibrations down my spine
Dare I ask why…

Lips in full bloom
Lotus flowers bow down to her grace
Back arched as he traces her eyes
Moist panties
Wet thighs
Musk scented lace
Devour him

Kneel at my waist
Give in to the taste
Your hand is your slave
Why do you wait

What is your fear
Quiet while I'm near
Shall I disappear
Then you'll never know

Your wisdom crept quietly
Like a kimono wrapped in sacred ceremony
Brooding eyes follow me
I bow to no one

Your honors weak
So vague when you speak
Why such riddles
I'm ancient text
Discover me

You are not my dream
Thou shall not weep
I am inertia
I am the sky
I am the one
That caught your eye
Go to sleep

Succubus
I do not trust
Encased in fever
It feeds the lust
You are not my dream
Don't flatter me
With idealisms
Or false honesty
Just go to sleep

Hot stones burn under foot
Walking toward contemplation
Blissful feelings
Honest thinking
Along the shoreline

Wandering days are a state of mind
Not looking for a high
Your colors cast shadows that paint lost time
Have I lost sight of what's right
Answers escape me
I let you decide, where it goes from here
For now you disappear
Along the shoreline

What paints the summits of your mind
When sound is a diversion
How will you pass the time
Let your life pour over mine
What are you searching for
When you kneel to the sky
Solitudes wrapped you in whispers

In your secret scarlet lusting
Divulge so little while your slipping
You serpent lips are trembling
Stained is the skin
You wear with envy
Solitudes burned your door down

Naked statue, stare and weep
Eyes of marble, fall asleep
Waking hours, seeming deep
Solitude is your mistress

Two simple spheres
Were cut in half
Bound by the universe
Creation has no mercy
Each spinning towards the sun
Looking for it's equal

The galaxy was angry
Expelled them from the sky
When they fell to earth
Each had lost their light

Celestial beings
Once worshipped by the stars
Taken from the heavens
Forced to live like us
And half was torn apart

The universe forgave them
But left them there to heal
What was once
Two single spheres
Were bonded by ideals

It was simple to one
So many made fun
Was everything to me
Simpleminded words
Just to deal with the hurt
It's all I had
Not what I wanted to be

Held on by mercy
When life was slipping
My children's faces burned in my mind
And the pen lets me write
I scroll with blinding tears
In love and fear
Just one more paragraph
Go ahead and laugh
Mock my simplicity
Show me my stupidity
Tear me apart
But it was really from my heart

I prayed for an angel
Anything would do
To drown out the screams
The pain
And bad dreams

As the machines took my breath
I could not speak
I lay there weak
You helped me believe
With just a few words
Softly, like a lullaby

You will never know
How I almost let go
Somehow my angel
Helped me survive

So do as you must
Really I am no one
Just wanted to say thank you
And move on

What seemed like years
Was a thought and a day
Do not question me
I have no answers
Stay on your safe side
With the sun in your eyes
Left yourself open
Just take your time

What held you back
Was a fear of falling
Do not follow me
I am not your calling
Stay on your road
With the sun in your mind
Left yourself hoping
But the words are mine

This is the brightest part of life
This is the moment when you know
You only heal
When you let go
This is who I am

What became of it all
Was everything destroyed
Do not question me
The answers are a void
Stay on the safe side
With the sky in your eyes
This is the time
It was always the time

This is the brightest part of life
This is the moment when you know
You only heal
When you let go
This is who I am

Monochromatic lust
Tracing syllables
With your tongue to your lips
Let your mind slip
Voyeur

Your picture mind haze
Fed with phrase
Say nothing
Just wonder
Voyeur

Monotonous hours
Idle hands
Seek refuge
Eyes shut
Thoughts thrust
Voyeur

Hidden skeptic
Fingers tremble
Quench your thirst
For answers
Voyeur

Wind of change blows my way
She entwines her eclectic bliss
With my every breath
She brings me serenity

Does she follow me
I whisper my envy to her
Secretly, I want to see her
She spirals in silence
I am at her mercy

You can only believe
Because time never ends
If you cannot see
How could it be
I hear her smile
Still she covers me

Wind of change
Bare your fruits
Show me mercy
And I'll follow you

You made me a mess
Never let up
You put me under a microscope
Always wanting me to please
The person I want to be

You dump on me
Constantly
Your wants
Your needs
I live
In simplicity

Then when your done
You expect me to run to you
When you've made me feel bad
When your done with being mad
You expect me to agree
With everything you see

I exist with a purpose
I am not worried
If it fits
With what you insist
Always trying to change me
Dress me
Or confess to me, I am not worthy
Torture me
Endlessly
Drain my humanity
Why not just go away
And set me free

My window
Safe haven
Looking towards heaven
Picture frame for the world
Many times I stare through your pane
Seeing my reflection
What a contradiction
You are my protection
From the elements of life

Rocks shatter your glass
They lay at my feet
Reminding me
Nothing is that easy

So hard to swallow
To fast to follow
Deny the feeling
Keeps you guessing
Lethargic screaming
Has no meaning
Are you seeing
What I see

Hail to your ego
Makes me sick
Your no better than me
And falling quick
I'm not your challenge
Your not my twist
You live in a box
Your head is a mess
Taste my kiss

These are the lips
Of reality
They won't spew worship
You won't find that in me
I see right through
Your society smile
Don't burn your bridges
While your worlds on fire

What I have been looking for
I'll never find it here
This place has left my eyes wide open
Blinded by ideals
With every word I feel secluded
Tarnished by the fire
Human natures always learning
Keeps us all inspired

Find your faith
What ever it takes
What makes you break
Will give you strength
Nothing can be that shallow
(Fall if you have to)
Redeemed

Looking for a quick release
The words become your fate
The paper never gives you mercy
It's all how you relate
Blinded by an indiscretion
Blinded by ideals
When every step you take is empty
You'll have to hurt to feel
(Again)

Find your faith
What ever it takes
What makes you break
Will give you strength
Nothing can be that shallow
(Fall if you have to)
Redeemed

What does the dark reveal to you
What do the whispers mean to you
Does the taste of wonder
Salivate your mouth
Does it rush your blood
Does it make you sweat
When you lay in bed
Do you think of what's said
Do you let it all out

What do the eyes tell you
Can you see it clear
Do you turn away
Play mind games
What will you do
When it disappears

What does it taste like
How would it feel
Could you handle it
Do you think it's real
This, you will never know

Look at this woman
Laying on the floor
Broken and torn
Years of hope
She wore
Like a coat of armor

She never let anyone know her
Where was the one to show her
How to love
Happy endings are not enough
To save her now
Head bowed down
She shakes and weeps
Covering eyes of glass
Hands of prayer
No ones there
To see

Look at this woman
The honest fear she keeps
Reaching for something to believe
So exhausted
So misguided
Seeking mercy

Look at this woman
Laying on the floor
A name, a face
No one

Welcome the warmth
Wrap prisms of color
Around your life
You are the wise
You are the light
Others will follow

Remember humility
Remember humanity
Be humble and smile
Your creativity feeds the soul
This will keep you whole
It's a long road to go
Know you'll be fine

Keep your insight
Trust your understanding
Show compassion
With open hands
Be the man
You believe in

Do not wait to speak
Silence will never give you mercy
Nothings what it seems
Beginnings are never easy
Rest assured
One simple word
Is all you need

Do not wait to connect
What slips by
Can torment your mind
Leave questions on your lips
Rest assured
It's not absurd
Go after it

Days so long and slipping
Moments lost
A severe cost
Never let you live it down....
Never know
Who wants to live like that

Do not wait to try
Own your life
Nothings going to change
Rest assured
No regrets
You will this time

A whisper
Makes you want to look into the eyes of the voice that
drips down your spine
Into your world
It feeds the imagination

A whisper covers your ears
In scarlet lusting
It seeps into your mind
Makes you crave touch
Whispers bare the hidden lust
They leave you waiting
With baited breath

Soft voice, caressing words
Test the tongue, challenge your will
Melodic temptation
Syllables linger in meditation on your soul
A whisper changes everything

Mint sensation
Warm vibrations
Flowing
Floating high above my head
It lifts me
It holds me
It takes me in

Surrender to the tingle
Makes the skin come alive
Eyes so bright
Eclectic insight
Waves of color
Canvas mind
Breathe and smile
Let go
Cinderella
Let go

I stood in the street, eyes straight ahead
The presence of people passing
Was like a whisper
The motion was slow, but lasted forever
Behind me, voices rolled off my mind
Humanity talking in tongues
Somehow I felt numb
Yet I made my way
Down the city's path

Never knowing what I might find
Never shaking the feeling I'd forget
North wind blows chills down my back
Whirlwinds of paper dance above my head
Traffic rushing, it echoes
While falling behind me now
My thoughts stretch
Wondering to where I am expected
What if I never show
What if I just keep going
Who would miss me
Now the raindrops kiss me
How the storm has blessed me
It made me stop
To take it all in
Life is telling me
This is it
The big bang
The real thing
You have been surviving
Better learn to live

Daybreak, paints shadows of red on your eye lids
Wake from the nocturnal bliss, of enchanted safety.
Touch my lips
With shallow breath
Air so pure, as the morning rises
Cotton comfort
Rest my weary head
In every moment
Silence is my lover
Crawling on my barren soul

So simple to let thought wash over you
A needed release
A promise to keep
Warm sun fall over me
From a window
From the sky
From my heart, to my mind
Let the day begin its journey

Run your hands down my body
Run your tongue across my lips
What's your twist
What makes you weak
So you cannot speak
Hands down my body
Run your tongue across my lips
What's your twist
What makes you weak
So you cannot speak
Give in to it

Eyes tell all
Rise and fall
When your that close
I feel the electricity
It over comes me

Up against the wall
Lets see you crawl
I know what you want
I know what I've got
My blood is hot
Do you challenge me

Can you take it
Lets not fake this
I want to taste it
So close to me

Does it make you sweat
When you know I'm wet
I'll tease you to death
But you'll feel so good.

Circle
Curves of endless perfection
We begin
We never end
As we follow the sphere
We will always meet

Like the rings in your eyes
We shine
Because will is everything
In the circle of light
Your soul is bright
And your love is endless

The hands of time
Remind us of empathy
Slowly creeping from behind
To make sure we see
Everything

This is how I feel you
Is this all a dream
This circle is a mystery
So healing
To bad you don't see me

The search was over
Truth be told
One day, one hour
Each word took hold
They hung to my thoughts
Waiting for resolve
I must move on

From the East of reason
To the West of understanding
Blown by the wind
Confused, but standing
I make my way
To the promised land

No need to behave
Get down and beg
Naughty boy
Lick my lips
I get my way

Look me up and down
Without a sound
Run my hands on your thighs
Make your zipper feel tight
Lets have fun tonight
Take me to bed

Pressed against my hips
Let my panties slip
Your now my toy
On your knees little boy
I know you enjoy it

Let your mind go numb
As I make you cum
I can taste your skin
Now I'm warm and wet
Twisted and perverted
Is your little secret

Beautiful, tranquil, honest kiss
Melt across my parted lips
Take my mind to tempting tides
You made this moment, burning bright
Show me what your world is like

Step outside this fateful day
Take this chance, that comes your way
Hold this hand with trembling hope
Breathe your words into my soul
Cast away the empty days
What you have, that stands before you
Will never slip away

Close your eyes
Let me paint your mind
Colors of gold and umber
Cast down from the trees
A gentle breeze
Crisp and inviting
Gone are the lazy days under the azure skies
Winter traces your lips with her smile
Just a kiss..
She leaves you waiting

Apple cider scented desires
Come closer to me
Wrap your woolen whispers round us
Autumn keeps us company
I think of you
As I drift to sleep

You are like liquid
Pour over my senses
Flow through my soul
Color my canvas

Touch is so healing
Release what your feeling
Dive into the music
Hold your breath
The melodies endless

You are like liquid
A sensual quenching
Spill into my daydreams
You keep me guessing

Moody and honest
Wise and charming
The flavor of peppermint
The color of morning
Shine down on me softly
With understanding

Shut and still
Took years to fill
Papers and pieces
From pockets or places
Hold on to their traces
Is just for security
Or for information

A drawer full of keep this
A place to put moments
Maybe I'll use it
But I'll hide it away
Never know where it went to
Till I clean it one day

Opened, I search it
Never know what I'll find
It's like looking through photos
In the back of your mind

The drawer's never empty
As much as I try
Keeps filling with maybe
Just like my life

This is samsara
Transitions nirvana
When you touch my mind
It's tantric euphoria

Watch, but don't speak
Want, but don't breathe
Prisms of water
Collect on your lips
This is the kiss
That starts your journey

Make your pilgrimage
From the dreams to the sky
Wondering why, this gets you so high
Similar minds
On the strangest days

Been riding out the blue tides
One day, runs to the next
Learned not to expect
No regrets
Keep moving forward
Never playing with "what if"

(chorus)
This is the strangest of days
Motivations empty
So set in my ways
Something's got to give
It helps to talk to you....

So numb to the echo's around me
Just voices gathering space
Lay around till the feeling is over
This is the only way I'll handle it..

(chorus)
This is the strangest of days
My motivation is empty
So set in my ways
I've got nothing to envy
Something's got to give
Then you smile at me..

These strange days
So long and lazy
The strangest things
Give me comfort

Feed lucid dreams
River of night
Wraps calm thoughts
In mud of sorrow
Weep, tree of woe
Your branches save this soul
From drowning

Forest of lost will
Dark earth under my foot
Moist from the rains of mercy
Bathe me in empathy
Whispers in misty halos
Fall from above my head
Pouring over me like a sacred sanctuary
I fall to my knees
Give in to thee
This is how to surrender

Celestial harmonies
Form above our heads
Music of the spheres
Spin light and understanding
Creativity is beyond what we see

As the spindle turns
The sirens of the heavens hum
Vibrating your soul, to the core
The most beautiful transition
A life could endure

Warm rays of tone and perfection
Octaves of nature, fall over us in grace
Intoxicating night, I feel you soar
Symphony of the universe
Heal me

Printed in the United States
67044LVS00002B/34